My Mind is a Mess

Julianna Jones

BookLeaf
Publishing

Presentation by *BookLeaf Publishing*

Web: www.bookleafpub.com

E-mail: info@bookleafpub.com

ISBN: 9789357613132

First edition 2022

Middle Child Mind set

Acting the oldest and always picked last, I had to learn to survive and do it fast. Never given the attention needed, so to independence I quickly conceded. It was always said I required less because I was more mature, but with how young I was treated I can't really be sure. I just wanted the same love I always though I was denied, it only made me feel worse when I was brushed aside. Maybe now that I'm older I can finally put to rest the middle child mind set.

Bundle of Nerves

My hands shake and I feel my brittle bones quake as I tap my fingers to the rhythm of thoughts in my head. Chewing the skin off the corner of my lips in hopes to quell the feelings of unease permeating from the back of my mind and into the rest of my body. Slowly devouring me until there is nothing left.

Bitter

A common taste that sits heavy on my tongue,
and has wormed its way into my heart. As the
feeling of it slowly tries to tear my soul apart.

Commitment Issues

Any relationships I've built have turned to ash, and any built in the future will surely crash. Cutting people off always seems rash, but my peace and stability never seem to last. Before I develop attachments I have to make my exit fast. I can't afford the casualties that would pile up after the blast, and when I'm alone I can finally breathe at last.

Mommy Issues

I couldn't love him in order for you to love me, the need for your approval just wouldn't let me be. I made myself lie so you would be pleased. As I got older I thought I could finally feel at ease, but I quickly learned my DNA chains you to me.

I Can't Be Suicidal

I held my breathe hoping I'd forget how to
breathe, and constantly wished for a permanent
sleep.
 If I said it out loud you would send me away; so
I cry at night and hide during the day.
 I'd write letters just to throw them away, and do
other things to keep the thoughts at bay.

Self-love

I just wanted to be loved and at first that didn't
seem like to much to ask, but then I tried to love
myself and had to take a step back.
 My once poetic tongue turned sharper than an
axe; with words more dangerous than anthrax.
 My nature and my will to do good always seem
to clash, causing all my actions to seem brash.

Mirror

I look in the mirror and have to do a double take;
it isn't the mirror but my mind that breaks.
 Nightmares of you keep me awake, and
memories of the past make my head ache.
 But I'll stand in the mirror for as long as it
takes, until it isn't my mind that breaks.

To My Sister pt.1

You've been through so much, and you weren't allowed to complain. So you packed all your things and had to run away. They made you feel crazy, and wouldn't let the courts believe you were sane. All the pain you were in didn't register in my brain. You would try so hard only to be shamed, trying to find solace in people was always in vain.

To My Sister pt.2

The anger you held nearly drove you insane, and nobody would ever take the blame. They stood back and watched as you navigated hell, never bothering to open your cell. They would watch and laugh as you fell, so all of your secrets never felt safe to tell. When you were away I always prayed you were well, because I knew the horrors of the place that you dwelled.

 There's so much to say, but not enough space on a page to write. I need you to know it's okay to not be right. You no longer have to fight for a love they were never willing to give, and it's okay to be happy that you lived. You don't have to shoulder the guilt, or take all of the blame. I'll always be here to listen even for petty complaints. You've taken on so much, and given it your best. Now just sit back it's finally safe to rest.

Liberty

There's a weight on my chest was I supposed to
feel blessed,
my body not my choice this world is a mess.
 Keep my mouth wired closed, and my legs tied
shut,
I'm allowed to complain about everything but.
 As my rights are stripped and my hands are
bound, I'm not allowed to stand my ground.
 How proud liberty stands, but is no where to be
found.
 Instead we keep our heads down as a means to
survive, in the land of the free no one can thrive.
 Our backs to the wall and rifles aimed high,
where all the living come to die.
 When it doesn't affect you it's easy to let it be,
but you don't know what the rest of us see.
 This land is not free, and if ever it was it wasn't
for me.

Regret

I can't bring myself to face the ghost of my past,
though it seems spirits are what I attract.
 They send chills down my spine, and bring with
them a list of sins I tried to leave behind.
 When I think they're gone I'm immediately
filled with dread; they hang like a heavy burden
over my head.
I can't sleep them away, and they make
themselves known even on sunny days.

Fake It

I tried to talk but no one would listen; so I gave up speaking it seemed like a hopeless mission. That I wasn't equipped to handle, and left me with a hurt to which nothing could hold a candle.

So I faked a smile and told people what they wanted to hear; only to have my soul slowly disappear.

With every lie and I'll be fine, my heart would break and beg to resign.

Relatable

The things you've thought, I've felt them too.
You spent your days thinking no one knew.
Locked away, alone in you room; awaiting your
impending doom.
Never knowing what comes next, always
drowning in regret.

Chameleon

I never believed in shape shifters until I met you.
Then your true colors showed in bright hues. A
master of disguise,
never dawning the same mask twice. Not seeing
past your facade was my only vice. Two faced
with no shame, you always managed to shift the
blame. In your honey sweet voice a dangerous
lullaby. Your pathetic sorry's only used to pacify.
My ears still burn from all your sweet lies. None
of it was ever true like all of your goodbyes.

Anxiety

It's like a mirror, the longer I stare the more
flaws I find. The more anxious the thought the
harder my teeth grind. I can't shake the feeling
that my hands are bound, and every where I look
there's no help to be found. My mind feels like it
stays in a fog, and keeps a permanent clog.
Every time I start to think I feel myself begin to
shrink.

Crisis of Faith

What do I do when forgiveness run out, and
every where I look love is in a drought? How do
I see beyond my own doubt? Religion seems to
leave a few key points out.
 Why am I expected to preach a message I have
trouble believing myself, or tell people in love
they are gonna burn in hell? How are you
demonstrating love when you are clearly filled
with hate? There's so many wrongs to make
right I hope we're not to late.

Vicious Cycle

I'm not surprised, this happens every time. You
use your crocodile tears, and then anger to instill
fear. You spout pretty word for others to hear,
but behind closed doors your mood shifts gears.
The pressures on though and your facade is
beginning to crumble. Soon all that will be left is
a pile of ruble. Then everyone will finally see
the vicious cycle in which you've trapped me.

Identity Crisis

I can't wait to finally be me, then maybe I won't feel as crazy as I seem. I'm not quite sure where I begin and the false personas start, but a lot of things are gonna crumble when I pull the knots apart.

The threads wrap around me, choking me until I can't breathe. I don't know if the madness will ever let me be. The task seems daunting now but once it is complete, I'll no longer be snared in a web of deceit.

Pessimism

Good days are a blessing, and bad ones feel like
a curse. Sometimes they're so muddled you don't
know which is worse.
  You can puff out your chest and stick up your
nose, but the past follows wherever you go.
  Energy is fleeting during the day, but you'll be
restless all night. Praying that monsters who
don't even exist won't come out to bite.
  You'll cry and beg for peace of mind, but
madness and insanity will be all you find.

Closing Statement

I've walked through life always looking over my shoulder. I could never bring myself to live a little bolder. Who knows maybe things will change now that I'm older. Hopefully I won't grow any colder.